Recipe Diary

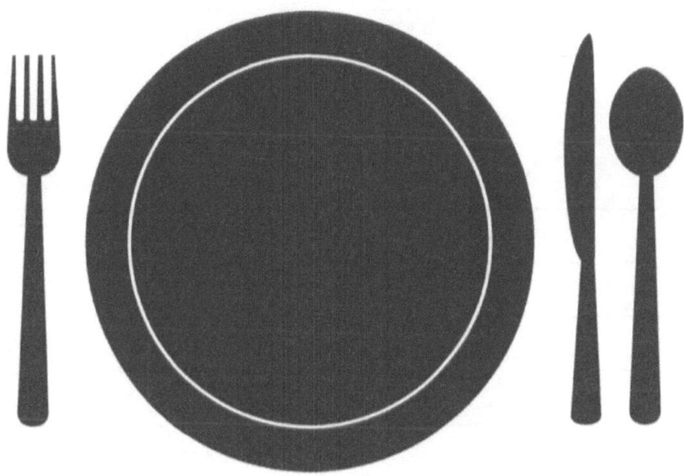

Recipe for

....

....

Cook Time ....*Serves* ....

Ingredients

Procedure

....

....

Cook Time ....Serves ....

Ingredients

Procedure

....

....

Cook Time ....*Serves* ....

Ingredients

Procedure

Recipe for

....

....

Cook Time ....Serves ....

Ingredients

Procedure

....

....

Cook Time ....Serves ....

Ingredients

Procedure

Recipe for

....

....

Cook Time ....*Serves* ....

Ingredients

____

____

____

____

____

____

Procedure

____

....

....

Cook Time ....Serves ....

Ingredients

Procedure

....

....

Cook Time ....Serves ....

Ingredients

Procedure

....

....

Cook Time ....Serves ....

Ingredients

Procedure

Recipe for

....

....

Cook Time ....*Serves* ....

Ingredients

___________________________   ___________________________

___________________________   ___________________________

___________________________   ___________________________

___________________________   ___________________________

___________________________   ___________________________

___________________________   ___________________________

___________________________   ___________________________

Procedure

Ingredients

___________________________   ___________________________

___________________________   ___________________________

___________________________   ___________________________

___________________________   ___________________________

___________________________   ___________________________

___________________________   ___________________________

Procedure

....

....

Cook Time ....*Serves* ....

Ingredients

_____________________________ _____________________________

Procedure

....

....

Cook Time ....Serves ....

Ingredients

Procedure

Ingredients

Procedure

Recipe for

....

....

Cook Time ....*Serves* ....

Ingredients

Procedure

Recipe for

....

....

Cook Time ....*Serves* ....

Ingredients

Procedure

....

....

Cook Time ....*Serves* ....

Ingredients

Procedure

Recipe for

....

....

Cook Time ....*Serves* ....

Ingredients

_____________________________   _____________________________

_____________________________   _____________________________

_____________________________   _____________________________

_____________________________   _____________________________

_____________________________   _____________________________

_____________________________   _____________________________

Procedure

____

____

____

____

____

____

____

____

____

____

____

____

____

....

....

Cook Time ....Serves ....

Ingredients

_____________________   _____________________

_____________________   _____________________

_____________________   _____________________

_____________________   _____________________

_____________________   _____________________

_____________________   _____________________

Procedure

____

____

____

____

____

____

____

____

____

____

____

____

____

____

Recipe for

....

....

Cook Time ....*Serves* ....

Ingredients

Procedure

Ingredients

Procedure

....

....

Cook Time ....Serves ....

Ingredients

_______________________________   _______________________________

_______________________________   _______________________________

_______________________________   _______________________________

_______________________________   _______________________________

_______________________________   _______________________________

_______________________________   _______________________________

_______________________________   _______________________________

Procedure

____

____

____

____

____

____

____

____

____

____

____

____

____

Recipe for

....

....

Cook Time ....*Serves* ....

Ingredients

Procedure

....

....

Cook Time ....Serves ....

Ingredients

_______________________________   _______________________________
_______________________________   _______________________________
_______________________________   _______________________________
_______________________________   _______________________________
_______________________________   _______________________________
_______________________________   _______________________________

Procedure

____
____
____
____
____
____
____
____
____
____
____
____
____

Cook Time ....Serves ....

Ingredients

Procedure

Recipe for

....

....

Cook Time ....*Serves* ....

Ingredients

___________________________   ___________________________

___________________________   ___________________________

___________________________   ___________________________

___________________________   ___________________________

___________________________   ___________________________

___________________________   ___________________________

Procedure

Cook Time ....Serves ....

Ingredients

Procedure

....

....

Cook Time ....Serves ....

Ingredients

Procedure

Recipe for

....

....

Cook Time ....*Serves* ....

Ingredients

Procedure

Ingredients

Procedure

....

....

Cook Time ....Serves ....

Ingredients

Procedure

Cook Time ....**Serves** ....

Ingredients

Procedure

Ingredients

Procedure

....

....

Cook Time ....Serves ....

Ingredients

Procedure

Recipe for

....

....

Cook Time ....Serves ....

Ingredients

Procedure

Ingredients

Procedure

....

....

Cook Time ....Serves ....

Ingredients

Procedure

Cook Time ....Serves ....

Ingredients

Procedure

Cook Time ....Serves ....

Ingredients

Procedure

Recipe for

....

....

Cook Time ....*Serves* ....

Ingredients

Procedure

....

....

Cook Time ....Serves ....

Ingredients

Procedure

Recipe for

....

....

Cook Time ....*Serves* ....

Ingredients

Procedure

....

....

Cook Time ....*Serves* ....

Ingredients

Procedure

....

....

Cook Time ....*Serves* ....

Ingredients

Procedure

....

....

Cook Time ....Serves ....

Ingredients

Procedure